24
Ready-to-Go
Genre Book Reports

by Susan Ludwig

SCHOLASTIC
PROFESSIONAL BOOKS

NEW YORK • TORONTO • LONDON • AUCKLAND • SYDNEY
MEXICO CITY • NEW DELHI • HONG KONG • BUENOS AIRES

To Roger

Cover design by Norma Ortiz
Interior design by Solutions by Design

ISBN: 0-439-23469-7

2 3 4 5 6 7 8 9 10   40   09 08 07 06 05 04 03

Contents

Introduction

Add pizzazz to your independent reading program with *24 Ready-to-Go Genre Books Reports*! This all-in-one resource helps students reflect meaningfully on popular genres: biography, memoir, fiction, science fiction, fantasy, nonfiction, mystery, and historical fiction. With several projects for each genre, this book will easily take you and your students through the school year. Although these projects are designed for particular genres, they are flexible enough to be used with any genre and any book.

These engaging projects move beyond traditional book report formats and challenge students to use their critical thinking skills and creativity. They'll nominate a character for president, design a cereal box, interview the main character, draw a comic strip, create a time capsule, and much more.

Designed for kids of all learning styles, the projects build essential reading and writing skills. Students strengthen reading comprehension as they analyze literary elements such as character, setting, plot, conflict, resolution, symbolism, point of view, and dialogue. They'll also build writing skills as they write and revise news articles, diary entries, letters, directions, movie scripts, and more.

Everything you need is included to implement the projects instantly and easily. For each project, you'll find:

- ☼ A **teacher page** that describes the project and provides helpful ideas to introduce and implement it

- ☼ Reproducible **student directions** that take the kids through each step of the project, from brainstorming to putting on the final touches

- ☼ A reproducible **evaluation rubric** that outlines the evaluation criteria and can be filled in by the student, teacher, or both

These hands-on book reports are sure to enhance any genre study and engage students as they reflect upon their independent reading. We hope that *24 Ready-to-Go Genre Book Reports* will help students enjoy both reading and responding to a wide range of literature.

The projects in this book can be used in a number of ways. Some suggestions are listed below, but feel free to adapt them to meet the needs of your students, schedule, and curriculum.

Genre of the Month

One way to organize your genre study is to introduce a "Genre of the Month." Introduce the genre with a discussion about its characteristics. Have students brainstorm a list of characteristics and add to it as needed. Ask students to name books they've read that fit into this genre. Invite a school librarian to give a book talk that features books in the genre and then add these and other books to a classroom display. Choose short passages to read aloud to the class.

Assigning the Projects

After assigning a genre for the month, give students due dates for the following three tasks: book approved, book read, and project finished. A week is a suggested time frame for finding a book and having it approved. If your class does not have an assigned day to visit the school library, you may want to schedule a time. The process of approving students' book selections will run more smoothly if you are there when students are choosing their books. As you are approving book selections, make sure that the books interest students and are at appropriate reading levels for them.

There are several ways you can use the projects. You might assign the same project for the entire class. Or you might allow students to choose from two to four projects. If a book deals with a serious topic, such as slavery or the Holocaust, students will need your guidance in selecting an appropriate project (for example, the comic strip report is not recommended). Please note that although the projects are designed for a particular genre, you can use the projects for other genres as well.

Refer to the teacher pages for suggestions on introducing each project. These pages provide discussion topics that will help students become interested in the project and help them get started. Before photocopying the student directions, review them and adapt if necessary. You may want to add or delete steps, depending upon the needs of your students and the amount of time students will have to complete a project.

Please note that the materials listed for each project usually do not specify exact sizes for paper and other supplies. If you would like projects to fit a specific size requirement, write this on the student directions sheet before photocopying it.

Next, distribute photocopies of the student directions. Have students write their name and fill in the three due dates in the box at the top of the page. They will then write the book title and author in step 1. Explain that these sheets provide directions for the project and questions that will help students brainstorm ideas for their work. Also explain that students should write neatly on these sheets because they will turn them in with their final project. Remind students that their final grade will be based on their work throughout the process, not just on the final project, so they should not skip any of the steps. It is also helpful to distribute copies of the rubric at this time so that students know the criteria on which they will be evaluated.

If you feel students need extra guidance in completing their projects, allow class time for students to work on them. In advance, remind students to bring their books and materials to school so that everyone will use this time effectively. This is a good opportunity to make sure that students understand the assignment and that they are on schedule.

Sharing and Displaying Finished Projects

The creative nature of the projects makes them interesting to share in classroom presentations, visual displays, or both. For example, students can present their fiction cereal box reports in the form of a commercial, read aloud their picture books to younger students, and act out their character interviews with a partner. Suggestions for how students can present their work to their classmates are included in the teacher pages. Since many of the projects include both writing and art, they make wonderful genre study bulletin board displays.

Assessing Student Work

Each project comes with its own reproducible rubric. Points are given for completion of each major step in the process and for general thoughtfulness, accuracy, and neatness. The points for each project add up to 100. If giving letter grades, let students know in advance the point range for each grade (for example, 90–100 is an A).

The reproducible rubric can be filled in by the teacher, student, or both. If both teacher and student will fill in the rubric, make two copies of it. Give one to the student and keep the other. Schedule a time to discuss each student's evaluation. Note any specific comments at the bottom of the form. If you would like to create your own rubric, photocopy and fill in the blank form on page 95. In addition, you'll find a reproducible reading log on page 96 on which students can keep a record of the books they've read.

Presidential Poster

┤ GUIDELINES ├

Objective: Students read a biography or memoir and nominate that individual for president. They then create a campaign poster that describes the candidate's qualities and background.

(NOTE: If the subject of the biography was actually president at one time, students can still complete this project.)

Posters should include the following:

☼ the traits and qualities that make this person a good leader

☼ information about the person's background (such as family, education, hometown, and so on)

☼ leadership experience (such as jobs or other accomplishments)

☼ a drawing or photograph of the person

You might show students examples of real campaign posters. Have students describe the design and writing style of the posters. Ask them what information is included and what might be added.

After students present their completed posters to the class, hold a mock presidential election. The completed posters make a nice display for the classroom and surrounding hall areas.

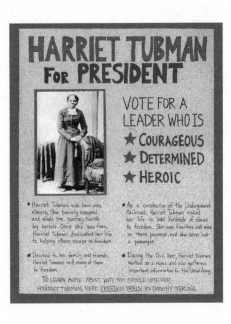

Name: _____ Date: _____

Presidential Poster

Imagine that the subject of your book has decided to run for president and has asked you to create a campaign poster. Look back through the book and think about whether or not the subject of the biography or memoir would make a good candidate for president. What qualities and characteristics would make this person a good leader? What leadership experience has this person had?

DUE DATES

Book approved

_____

Book finished

_____

Project finished

_____

MATERIALS

posterboard or large sheet of construction paper, markers or crayons, glue, scissors, colored construction paper, pictures of the person for reference

DIRECTIONS

(1) Find a biography or memoir that interests you and is at an appropriate reading level for you. Have your book approved by your teacher.

Book Title: _____

Author: _____

(2) Look through the book and take notes about the subject of your book. List some adjectives that describe the person. Beside each adjective, write something the person did or said that shows that characteristic or quality.

_____

_____

_____

_____

(3) Think about what experience the person has had that would prepare him or her for the role of president. List the experiences along with any reasons this would be good preparation for a president.

_____

_____

_____

(4) Think about what information you will include on the campaign poster. Write a rough draft in a style that is upbeat and persuasive. Include the following information:

- ✿ person's name in large letters (for example, "Harriet Tubman for President")
- ✿ hometown
- ✿ family
- ✿ education
- ✿ work experience
- ✿ personal characteristics
- ✿ what this person might accomplish as president
- ✿ a photo or drawing of the person

(5) Sketch the design of the poster. Decide how you will fit all the information and what size it should be. Think about how you can make the poster colorful and attractive.

(6) Now you're ready to make your poster. In pencil, transfer the information from your rough draft to posterboard or a large sheet of construction paper. Color your poster and then draw a picture of the person (or attach a photo).

(7) Present your campaign poster to the class. Plan what you will say to try to convince your classmates to vote for your candidate.

Name: _____   Date: _____

Biography/Memoir

Presidential Poster

Book Title: _____

	POSSIBLE POINTS	POINTS EARNED
1 Was your book approved by the due date?	5	
2 Did you hand in your project on time?	10	
3 Was your poster neat, colorful, and attractive?	15	
4 Did you include thoughtful and convincing information about the person?	35	
5 Was the information complete?	20	
6 Are the spelling, punctuation, and grammar correct?	10	
7 Was your presentation informative and convincing?	5	

Comments: _____

_____

_____

_____

_____

_____

_____

24 Ready-to-Go Genre Book Reports ✳ Scholastic Professional Books

Diary Entry

GUIDELINES

Objective: *Students choose three important events from their biography or memoir. For each event, students write a one-page diary entry from the point of view of the subject of the book.*

Explain to students that they will write diary entries about three important events in their book. The dates students choose do not need to be consecutive. They can write about three events that took place at any point in the person's life.

Show students examples of diary entries from other books. Discuss point of view to ensure that students understand what it means to write in first person. Discuss how students might elaborate on the events they will describe. Write the following questions on the board:

* What were the person's observations of the events?

* How did the person feel about the events?

* What did the person learn from the events?

* What does the person hope the outcome of the events will be?

* What are the person's hopes for the future?

Explain that the entries should go beyond retelling the events. They should reflect the character's personality and should sound as if the character wrote them. Encourage students to look at dialogue in the book to understand how the character communicates and the kind of language he or she might use.

Have students create a cover for their diary entries and bind them together. Encourage them to decorate their diary covers in a way that reflects the person's personality and the time period in which he or she lived.

After students have finished their entries, ask them to choose their favorite one. Photocopy these entries and bind them into a class book, or have students read aloud their entries. Use each entry as a springboard for discussion about the subjects of the biographies. Encourage students to explain why they chose to share this particular entry. What do they hope their classmates will learn from it?

Biography/Memoir

Diary Entry

If the subject of your biography or memoir had kept a diary, what do you think he or she would have written about? Put yourself in the person's shoes for this assignment. Choose three important events from the person's life and write a one-page diary entry about each.

DUE DATES
Book approved
_____
Book finished
_____
Project finished
_____

| MATERIALS |

lined paper, construction paper, markers or crayons

| DIRECTIONS |

(1) Find a biography or memoir that interests you and is at an appropriate reading level for you. Have your book approved by your teacher.

Book Title: _____

Author: _____

(2) Look for important events that you might write about in your diary entries. Briefly describe each event and write the page numbers below.

1. _____
_____

2. _____
_____

3. _____
_____

4. _____
_____

5. _____
_____

(3) Review the list of events and circle three events you would like to write about.

24 Ready-to-Go Genre Book Reports ★ Scholastic Professional Books

❨4❩ Imagine that you are the person in the biography or memoir and that you have just experienced the first event. Think about how to describe this event from the character's perspective.

✿ How would the character describe what happened?

_____

_____

✿ What did the person see or hear?

_____

_____

✿ How did the person feel as the event was happening?

_____

_____

✿ How did the person feel once the event was over?

_____

_____

✿ How did other people react to the event?

_____

_____

❨5❩ Write a rough draft of the journal entry from the character's point of view. (This is called writing in first person.) Try to make the writing sound as if the character had written it. Think about the kind of language he or she would have used.

❨6❩ Write rough drafts of your diary entries for the other two events you chose. Look over the questions in step 4 to help you decide what to include.

❨7❩ Revise your writing and write a final draft.

❨8❩ Make a cover for the diary. Decorate the diary in a way that reflects the character's personality and the time period in which he or she lived. Write the person's name on it and your name below it.

Name: _____   Date: _____

Biography/Memoir

Diary Entry

Book Title: _____

	POSSIBLE POINTS	POINTS EARNED
(1) Was your book approved by the due date?	5	
(2) Did you hand in your diary on time?	10	
(3) Did you write three one-page diary entries?	30	
(4) Did you write about interesting or important events?	15	
(5) Did you write from the character's point of view?	15	
(6) Are the entries detailed and well written?	10	
(7) Are the spelling, punctuation, and grammar correct?	10	
(8) Did you make a cover for your diary?	5	

Comments: _____

_____

_____

_____

_____

_____

24 Ready-to-Go Genre Book Reports ✷ Scholastic Professional Books

Dress-Up Day

GUIDELINES

Objective: Students dress up as the subject of their biography or memoir and answer their classmates' questions in a brief presentation.

Post a list of the people whom students have read about. As a group, generate at least three questions for each of these famous people. You might have students work in small groups to come up with questions. Explain that a good question will reveal interesting and in-depth information. If a question requires a yes or no answer, have students add a second part to the question that asks the person to explain his or her response.

Give students suggestions for questions, such as:

✸ Which of your accomplishments gives you the greatest sense of pride and why?

✸ What was the greatest challenge you faced? How did you deal with it?

✸ What advice would you give students our age?

✸ Is there anything else that you wished you had accomplished?

✸ Who were your role models and why?

✸ What do you hope people will remember about you?

Have students write each question on an index card with the famous person's name at the top. Distribute the questions to the appropriate students so that they can research the answers. If students can't find the answers, they should use what they know about the person to come up with a response.

Explain that students should look up information in their book about how their character looked and dressed. Each student will dress up as the character on his or her assigned day and present a five-minute speech, role-playing the character. You may wish to stagger presentations over a period of a week or more. In their presentations, students should answer the questions from their classmates and present additional information. Discuss other information students might include, such as family history, important accomplishments, and so on.

If students have difficulty obtaining an appropriate costume, have them instead draw a large, colorful illustration of what the person would have worn. Display the sketch beside the student as he or she is presenting.

Name: _____ Date: _____

Biography/Memoir

Dress-Up Day

Imagine that the person you read about walked into your classroom and introduced himself or herself. What would he or she say? How would the person talk, act, and dress? For this project, you will prepare a short presentation as if you are the subject of your biography or memoir. In your presentation, you will answer questions that your classmates have about this person.

MATERIALS

clothing that the subject of the book might have worn (or drawing materials to illustrate this), index cards

DIRECTIONS

(1) Find a biography or memoir that interests you and is at an appropriate reading level for you. Have your book approved by your teacher.

   Book Title: _____

   Author: _____

(2) Read the questions that your classmates prepared. Write the answers on the index cards. If you do not know an answer, use what you know about the person to guess how he or she might have responded.

(3) Take notes on the subject of your book. Include information about the following:

   ✿ family

   _____

   _____

   ✿ hometown

   _____

   _____

   ✿ date of birth (and death, if applicable)

   _____

   _____

24 Ready-to-Go Genre Book Reports ✳ Scholastic Professional Books

✹ personality and character traits

_____

_____

✹ important accomplishments

_____

_____

✹ goals

_____

_____

✹ obstacles

_____

_____

✹ major events in the person's life

_____

_____

✹ contributions to society

_____

_____

❆4❆ Write a one-page monologue that you will present to the class. Write as if you are the person talking about himself or herself—for example, "I was born in 1877." Incorporate the information from your notes as well as the answers to your classmates' questions.

❆5❆ Read your monologue aloud and then revise it. Time yourself presenting your speech and make sure it takes about five minutes. Revise as necessary. Write your final draft neatly on index cards. You will turn in your index cards, so write your name or initials on each one.

❆6❆ Practice your speech so that you do not need to read from the index cards. (You may refer to them, but you should be able to make eye contact for most of your presentation.) Practice speaking and acting as you imagine the person would have.

❆7❆ Find out what the person looked like and how he or she dressed. On the day of your presentation, you will either dress in a costume to look like the person or bring in a large, colorful picture of him or her that you've drawn.

Name: _____ Date: _____

Biography/Memoir

Dress-Up Day

Book Title: _____

	POSSIBLE POINTS	POINTS EARNED
1 Was your book approved by the due date?	5	
2 Did you hand in your index cards on time?	10	
3 Was your presentation clear and easy to understand?	10	
4 Was your presentation informative?	20	
5 Did you answer your classmates' questions?	15	
6 Did you act like the character during your presentation?	10	
7 Did you dress as the character or draw a picture?	10	
8 Did you make eye contact for most of your presentation?	10	
9 Are the spelling, punctuation, and grammar correct?	10	

Comments: _____

_____

_____

_____

24 Ready-to-Go Genre Book Reports ✳ Scholastic Professional Books

Time Capsule

GUIDELINES

Objective: *Students create a time capsule that represents the subject of a biography or memoir and write an explanation for each object they include.*

Start by discussing objects that are significant to students. Help students to understand the difference between objects they like (video games, shoes, and so on) and objects that might have a deeper meaning for them. Explain that a symbol is an object that represents something important. It symbolizes something else that is more significant than the object itself.

Explain that students will imagine that they are the subjects of their books and that they will create a time capsule about the person. They should put themselves in the person's shoes and ask themselves what they would like future generations to learn about them. Then, they will choose objects that represent important information about the person. Students will also write a brief paragraph explaining why they included each object. They should write in the first person, as if they are the characters—for example, "I included this letter from my best friend to show how important friendships are to me."

Explain that time capsules are more fun to open if they include actual objects, but students should not include objects that are valuable. If they cannot find a particular object, students can draw a picture instead.

Students will decorate a shoe box to represent the person. They will store the objects and explanations inside. For a class activity, divide the class into small groups. Pass the time capsules around for each group to open and read. After a few minutes, have each group put everything back in the time capsule and pass it to the next group.

Biography/Memoir

Time Capsule

Imagine that the subject of your book made a time capsule to let future generations know about his or her life. What would the person have included? Create a time capsule and write a brief description of each item inside.

┇ MATERIALS ┇

shoe box, white construction paper, 3- by 5-inch index cards, markers or colored paper, found objects

┇ DIRECTIONS ┇

(1) Find a biography or memoir that interests you and is at an appropriate reading level for you. Have your book approved by your teacher.

Book Title: _____

Author: _____

(2) Brainstorm a list of important people, places, objects, and events in the person's life.

_____

_____

_____

_____

(3) Imagine that you are that person and you are creating a time capsule. Refer to the list from the previous question to give you ideas about the objects you might include. The objects you choose can represent the people, places, and events that were important to the person. They can also represent the person's interests or aspects of his or her personality. You may include actual objects or drawings of them if the objects are unavailable. Include at least five objects or drawings.

(4) For each item, write a short paragraph from the character's perspective about why you included it. Write each explanation on an index card and attach it to the appropriate object.

(5) Decorate a shoe box in a way that represents the subject of your biography. You might cover it in paper and draw on it, glue pictures on it like a collage, or otherwise decorate it. Write the title, author, and your name on the box.

DUE DATES

Book approved

_____

Book finished

_____

Project finished

_____

Name: _____ Date: _____

Biography/Memoir

Time Capsule

Book Title: _____

	POSSIBLE POINTS	POINTS EARNED
❀1❀ Was your book approved by the due date?	5	
❀2❀ Did you hand in your project on time?	10	
❀3❀ Did you make a list of important people, places, objects, and events?	10	
❀4❀ Did you include at least five objects or drawings in your time capsule?	20	
❀5❀ Did the objects represent important information about the person?	20	
❀6❀ Did you write at least five thoughtful explanations?	15	
❀7❀ Did you decorate your shoe box and write the title, author, and your name on it?	10	
❀8❀ Are the spelling, punctuation, and grammar correct?	10	

Comments: _____
_____
_____
_____
_____

A New Cereal on the Shelf

GUIDELINES

Objective: Students invent a cereal based on a fictional book and design a cereal box that presents information about the story in a fun, creative format.

The guidelines for each part of the cereal box are as follows:

✿ **Front**

Students write the name of their cereal and draw an illustration. Encourage students to think of a fun and enticing name—for example, for *Harry Potter and the Sorcerer's Stone*, they might invent a cereal called Wizard's Wands, a toasted oat cereal in the shape of lightning bolts. Explain that the name and shape of the cereal should relate to their books. Point out the various characters, logos, and other elements on actual cereal boxes. Encourage students to make their cereal box look like a real product while relating it to the book. Discuss the colors and style of text and the use of "bursts" to include additional information. Explain that the purpose of these elements is to entice consumers to buy the product.

✿ **Back**

Students design a game that is based on the story. It can be a puzzle, a word game, or any other fun activity that might be found on the back of a cereal box. Discuss ways that students can incorporate information from their book into their game. They might include information about the characters, setting, plot, and so on.

✿ **Right Side**

Under the heading "Ingredients," students list the main characters and write a sentence about each one. They also write a sentence or two about the setting.

✿ **Left Side**

Students write a summary that describes the main conflict and the resolution of the book. Discuss ways to make the language sound appealing, as if they are advertising the book.

✿ **Top**

Students write the title and author of the book and their name.

Finally, students plan a two-minute commercial advertising their cereal and present it to the class.

Fiction

A New Cereal on the Shelf

If you could invent a cereal based on the fictional book you read, what would it be? After you think of a name and shape for your cereal, you'll design a cereal box for it.

DUE DATES

Book approved

_____

Book finished

_____

Project finished

_____

| MATERIALS }

empty cereal box, white or light-colored paper, scissors, markers or crayons, construction paper, glue, tape

| DIRECTIONS }

(1) Find a fictional book that interests you and is at an appropriate reading level for you. Have your book approved by your teacher.

Book Title: _____

Author: _____

(2) Think about what you will name your cereal. Choose a name that sounds enticing and that relates to the story in some way. Then, choose a shape for the cereal, as well as colors and ingredients that also relate to the book. For example, for *Harry Potter and the Sorcerer's Stone*, you might invent a cereal called Wizard Wands, a toasted oat cereal in the shape of a miniature lightning bolts.

(3) Cover an empty cereal box with white or light-colored paper. Or you might want to write and draw on appropriate-sized sheets of paper and then glue them onto the box. Write a rough draft and draw sketches before moving on to your final copy. Here are the guidelines for each side of the box:

☼ **Front**

Write the name of your cereal and draw a picture to go with it. You might draw characters or other pictures to help sell your product. Make your cereal box look appealing and fun. Look at actual cereal boxes for ideas.

_____

_____

☼ **Back**

Design a game that is based on the story. It can be a puzzle, a word game, or any other fun activity that might be found on the back of a cereal box. Make sure it includes information from the book. Describe your idea below.

_____

Name: _____ Date: _____

_____

_____

_____

_____

☼ **Right Side**

Under the heading "Ingredients," list the main characters and write a sentence about each one. Then describe the setting (place and time). Write your rough draft below.

_____

_____

_____

_____

_____

_____

☼ **Left Side**

Write a summary of the book. Describe the main conflict and the resolution.

_____

_____

_____

_____

_____

☼ **Top**

Write the title and author of the book and your name.

❂4❂ Plan a two-minute commercial for your cereal, and present it to the class.

24 Ready-to-Go Genre Book Reports ✳ Scholastic Professional Books

Name: _____ Date: _____

Fiction

A New Cereal on the Shelf

Book Title: _____

	POSSIBLE POINTS	POINTS EARNED
(1) Was your book approved by the due date?	5	
(2) Did you hand in your project on time?	10	
(3) Is your cereal box neat, colorful, and attractive?	15	
(4) Is the front of the box complete and thoughtfully done?	10	
(5) Is the back of the box complete and thoughtfully done?	15	
(6) Is the right side complete and accurate?	10	
(7) Is the left side complete and accurate?	10	
(8) Is the top complete and accurate?	5	
(9) Are the spelling, punctuation, and grammar correct?	10	
(10) Was your commercial informative and interesting?	10	

Comments: _____

_____

_____

_____

The Main Character's in Town!

Objective: Students pretend to interview the main character of a fictional book for the local newspaper. Students generate at least five thoughtful questions and then answer them from the character's point of view.

Choose a book that the class has read. Together, brainstorm questions that an interviewer might ask the main character. Explain that a good question will require more than a yes or no answer. The character should always be asked to explain his or her answers. The questions should reveal the character's beliefs, hopes, goals, and aspects of his or her personality. Write the following prompts on the board:

✿ "How did you feel when…?"

✿ "What did you hope would happen when…?"

✿ "Why did you…?"

Next, explain that students will switch roles from that of the interviewer to the character being interviewed. Discuss point of view to ensure that students understand what it means to write in the first person. How do they think the character would answer the questions? Explain that they might not know exactly how the character would respond. Students should use what they know about the character to answer the questions. Encourage children to use information from the book to support their answers. Point out that there are many possible answers and that students should give reasons for their responses.

Have student pairs present the interviews to the class. Give students an opportunity to practice reading the interviews, with one student playing the interviewer and the other playing the character. Then have students read the interviews aloud to the class. You might also give students the option to read both parts of their interview, changing their voice to signal when they are the character and when they are the interviewer.

Fiction

The Main Character's in Town!

Imagine that you are a reporter for your local newspaper. The editor has just called to give you your latest assignment. You have been asked to interview a special visitor to your town—the main character of the book you just read!

DUE DATES

Book approved

_____

Book finished

_____

Project finished

_____

┃ MATERIALS ┃

lined paper

┃ DIRECTIONS ┃

(1) Find a fictional book that interests you and is at an appropriate reading level for you. Have your book approved by your teacher.

Book Title: _____

Author: _____

(2) Write a paragraph describing the main character of the story. Include the character's age, hometown, occupation, hobbies, personality traits, and so on.

Name: _____

Description: _____

_____

_____

_____

(3) Think about what you would like to ask the character and what the newspaper's readers would want to find out about him or her. Write at least five questions that will reveal interesting and important information about the character. Write the questions on the next page. If the question requires a yes or no answer, ask the character to explain his or her responses. Base some of the questions on events in the book, such as:

    ✿ "How did you feel when…?"

    ✿ "What did you hope would happen when…?"

    ✿ "Why did you…?"

✵(4)✵ After you have written the questions, put yourself in the character's shoes and write a rough draft of your answers on the lines labeled "Response." Use information from the story in the character's responses. If you need more room, use the back of this page or another sheet of paper.

Question 1: _____

_____

Response: _____

_____

Question 2: _____

_____

Response: _____

_____

Question 3: _____

_____

Response: _____

_____

Question 4: _____

_____

Response: _____

_____

Question 5: _____

_____

Response: _____

_____

✵(5)✵ Proofread your questions and answers and add any additional information that will make your writing stronger. Then write a final draft on a separate sheet of paper.

Name: _____   Date: _____

Fiction

The Main Character's in Town!

Book Title: _____

	POSSIBLE POINTS	POINTS EARNED
(1) Was your book approved by the due date?	5	
(2) Did you hand in your project on time?	10	
(3) Are your questions interesting and thoughtful?	25	
(4) Are your responses thoughtful and complete?	30	
(5) Did you write a rough draft?	10	
(6) Did you write a final draft with at least five questions and answers?	10	
(7) Are the spelling, punctuation, and grammar correct?	10	

Comments: _____

_____

_____

_____

_____

_____

_____

Write a Picture Book

Objective: Students write and illustrate a picture book based on a fictional book.

Display picture books in your classroom and encourage students to read them when they have finished a task or during a designated time. Draw students' attention to the writing style, simple language, dialogue, and illustrations that support the text. Ask them what they like about children's books and which are their favorites.

To prepare for this project, students first describe the beginning, middle, and ending of their book. This will help them identify the most important aspects to include in their children's book. After they have written summaries of each part, they write a rough draft of the children's book. Explain to students that they should refer to the summaries to help them retell the story, but that their stories should not merely summarize the events. Recall the children's books on display and the aspects that made the stories interesting. If students are having a difficult time with this assignment, have them retell just one chapter or episode from their book instead.

After students have written a rough draft, encourage them to revise. Then they can decide how they will arrange their book. They should plan to include about a paragraph of text on each $8\frac{1}{2}$- by $5\frac{1}{2}$-inch sheet of paper. Students may need to shorten their books if the text is running too long. Instruct them to write the text at the bottom of the page so that they can draw an illustration above.

Next, on each page, students draw and color an illustration that supports the text. Explain that this will help young readers understand the story. Have students add a cover with a title and illustration, arrange the pages in order, and staple along the left side.

Add these books to your children's book display. If possible, invite a first- or second-grade class to visit. Have students pair up with the younger children and read the books together.

Name: _____ Date: _____

Write a Picture Book

Have you ever wondered what it would be like to be a picture book author or illustrator? This activity will give you a chance to find out. Imagine that you are going to rewrite the book you just read for a first- or second-grade child. What are the most important events of the book? How could you describe them in a simple way?

DUE DATES
Book approved
_____
Book finished
_____
Project finished
_____

MATERIALS

$8\frac{1}{2}$- by 11-inch white construction paper (cut or folded in half to form $8\frac{1}{2}$- by $5\frac{1}{2}$-inch sheets), markers or crayons, stapler

DIRECTIONS

1 Find a fictional book that interests you and is at an appropriate reading level for you. Have your book approved by your teacher.

　　　Book Title: _____

　　　Author: _____

2 Write a brief summary of the beginning, middle, and ending of the book:

Beginning: _____

_____

_____

_____

_____

Middle: _____

_____

_____

_____

_____

_____

Name: _____ Date: _____

Ending: _____

_____

_____

_____

_____

(3) Read your summaries and think about how you can rewrite the information as a story for children. Write a rough draft of the story, using language that a first- or second-grade student could understand. (If you are having a difficult time simplifying the story, you might retell your favorite chapter or episode instead of the whole book.) Plan to include about a paragraph of text on each page. Include dialogue and some details to make the story interesting. Decide how you will illustrate each page. Revise your story to make your writing stronger.

(4) Transfer the story onto white paper. Draw and color a picture on each page.

(5) Add a cover and write the title of the book, your name, and the original author's name—for example: "Black Beauty," retold by (your name), original story by Anna Sewell. Draw and color a picture on the cover. Sketch the cover below before creating your final copy. Arrange the pages in order with the cover on top and staple along the left side.

24 Ready-to-Go Genre Book Reports ✳ Scholastic Professional Books

Name: _____ Date: _____

Fiction

Write a Picture Book

Book Title: _____

	POSSIBLE POINTS	POINTS EARNED
1 Did you have your book approved on time?	5	
2 Did you hand in your project on time?	10	
3 Did you write a paragraph summary of each part?	10	
4 Did you write a rough draft of your story?	10	
5 Did you revise?	10	
6 Did you complete your children's book?	25	
7 Is your project thoughtful and well written?	10	
8 Is your project neat, colorful, and attractive?	10	
9 Are the spelling, punctuation, and grammar correct?	10	

Comments: _____

_____

_____

_____

_____

Spend a Day

GUIDELINES

Objective: Students imagine that they are visiting the setting of the book and spending a day with one of the characters. Students describe three activities from their imaginary day and draw an illustration of each.

To help students choose a character as their tour guide, have them first make a list of the characters from the book and briefly describe each one. Students then imagine that they are visiting the setting of the book (this may involve time travel!), where they participate in three activities with the character. What activities do they think the character would choose? Encourage students to think about what there is to do in this place and time period.

Students write a one-page description of each activity. They should include their observations of the setting and their reactions to what they see and do. Encourage students to include some dialogue with their tour guide and any other characters they might meet. Then students draw and color an illustration for each activity and bind their pages together with a cover.

To give students an idea of what kind of activities they might choose, discuss a book you have read as a class. Choose a character as a tour guide, and then brainstorm activities that would lend themselves to an interesting description. You might write a paragraph together describing one of the activities. Challenge children to show aspects of the character's personality in their description. The description should give an impression not just of the activity but also of the time, place, and character.

Fiction

Spend a Day

What if you could spend the day in the setting of your book? Which character would you choose to be your tour guide? For this project, you'll describe three activities that you would do during your visit and draw a picture of each of them.

DUE DATES

Book approved

_____

Book finished

_____

Project finished

_____

| MATERIALS }

lined paper, unlined paper, crayons or colored pencils

| DIRECTIONS }

1) Find a fictional book that interests you and is at an appropriate reading level for you. Have your book approved by your teacher.

        Book Title: _Hatchet_____

        Author: _Gary Paulsen_____

2) Write a few sentences describing the setting (time and place) of the book.

_____

_____

_____

_____

_____

3) List the main characters and write a few sentences describing each one. Use another sheet of paper for additional space.

_____

_____

_____

_____

_____

_____

{4} Now look at your character list and circle the character that will be your tour guide.

Brainstorm Ideas

{5} Imagine that this character has planned three activities for you to do. What do you think he or she would choose? Consider the places in the book as well as the time period. Think about activities this character enjoyed in the book. Write three activities on the lines.

Do in class

1. _____

_____

2. _____

_____

3. _____

_____

minimum 10 sent.

{6} Write a one-page description of each activity for your rough draft. Describe what you saw and did, as well as your reactions to each activity. You might also include dialogue between you and the character. Did you meet any of the other characters?

{7} Draw and color an illustration to go with each activity. *detail, full page*

{8} Revise your writing, and write a final draft.

{9} Add a cover with a title (for example, "My Day With Jo," From *Little Women*). Write your name on the cover, and staple everything together.

24 Ready-to-Go Genre Book Reports ✸ Scholastic Professional Books

Name: _____ Date: _____

Fiction

Spend a Day

Book Title: _____

	POSSIBLE POINTS	POINTS EARNED
(1) Was your book approved by the due date?	5	
(2) Did you hand in your project on time?	10	
(3) Did you list and briefly describe the main characters?	10	
(4) Did you write a page about each activity?	30	
(5) Is your writing thoughtful and interesting?	20	
(6) Did you draw an illustration to accompany each activity?	10	
(7) Did you make a cover?	5	
(8) Are the spelling, punctuation, and grammar correct?	10	

Comments: _____

_____

_____

_____

_____

_____

Extra! Extra!

GUIDELINES

Objective: *Students write two newspaper articles based on a science fiction or fantasy book. In one article, students report an event that occurred in the book. In the other article, students report an event they made up based on the characters and story.*

Read aloud short news articles to give students an idea of their purpose and style. Write the following questions on the board, and explain that an article should answer all of them.

- ✹ Who?
- ✹ What?
- ✹ When?
- ✹ Where?
- ✹ Why?

Challenge students to underline the parts of the articles that answer these questions. Point out that they can usually find the answers at the beginning of an article. Ask students what additional information or details the reporter included. Look for direct quotations. Discuss the writing style of news articles, and have students notice that the sentences are usually succinct and to the point.

Explain that students will choose an exciting event from their book and write a newspaper article about it. Students will answer the five questions in their articles and then provide additional details, such as quotations, observations, and other details. Look at examples of headlines and then have children write a headline for their article.

Next, explain that students will make up an event that might have happened involving the characters in the book. The event could happen at any point in the story. Students will follow the same directions to write this article, again answering the five questions.

After students have written rough drafts of both articles, they write a final draft that looks like the front page of a newspaper. Have students draw an illustration for one of the articles and add a clever title that relates to the book.

Set up a newsstand in your classroom with the newspapers that students created. Encourage visitors and class members to read the newspapers on display. You might have students choose an article to read to the class.

Name: _____ Date: _____

Science Fiction/Fantasy

Extra! Extra!

For this project, you'll create the front page of a newspaper with two articles based on your science fiction or fantasy book. You'll report one event that happened in the story and one event that you've made up.

DUE DATES

Book approved

_____

Book finished

_____

Project finished

_____

MATERIALS

lined paper, a large sheet of unlined white paper, crayons or markers

DIRECTIONS

1. Find a science fiction or fantasy book that interests you and is at an appropriate reading level for you. Have your book approved by your teacher.

    Book Title: _____

    Author: _____

2. Think about the interesting events in the story. Choose one on which to base your article. To get started, answer the following questions about the event.

    Who? _____

    _____

    What? _____

    _____

    When? _____

    _____

    Where? _____

    _____

    Why? _____

    _____

3. On a separate sheet of paper, write a rough draft of your article. Give your article a headline.

{4} Think of an exciting event that could have happened in the book but did not. Your event could take place at any point in the story and should include actual characters and places from the book. Answer the following questions about your made-up event.

Who? _____

_____

What? _____

_____

When? _____

_____

Where? _____

_____

Why? _____

_____

{5} On a separate sheet of paper, write a rough draft of your article. Give your article a headline.

{6} Read your articles and revise to make your writing stronger and more interesting.

{7} Design a front page of a newspaper. Sketch it on scrap paper. Think of a title for your newspaper that relates to your book. Then, neatly copy each article onto the page. Draw a picture to illustrate one of the articles and write a caption beneath it (a sentence that describes the picture).

Name: _____ Date: _____

Science Fiction/Fantasy

Extra, Extra!

Book Title: _____

	POSSIBLE POINTS	POINTS EARNED
(1) Was your book approved by the due date?	5	
(2) Did you hand in your project on time?	10	
(3) Did you write two articles, one about an event in the book and one about an event you made up?	25	
(4) Did you answer the five questions in each article?	20	
(5) Was your writing thoughtful and interesting?	10	
(6) Did you write a headline for each article?	10	
(7) Did you draw a picture and write a caption for it?	10	
(8) Are the spelling, punctuation, and grammar correct?	10	

Comments: _____

_____

_____

_____

_____

Design a Game

GUIDELINES

Objective: Students create a board game based on a science fiction or fantasy book.

Display board games to give children ideas. You might set aside time for them to play the games. Lead a discussion about what makes a game fun and what elements a game might include, such as

- ☼ a game board
- ☼ clear and easy-to-follow directions
- ☼ a spinner or die
- ☼ cards
- ☼ playing pieces
- ☼ a fun name

Explain to students that a game should have a clear purpose and that students should determine how a player wins. Encourage students to keep their games as simple as possible. This will make it easier for them to write the directions and will also make the games more enjoyable to play. Show students examples of easy-to-follow directions for a simple game. Point out that the directions are numbered.

Show students how to make a simple spinner by using a paper clip and/or brass fastener.

 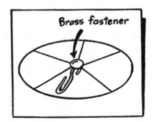

Discuss ways that students can incorporate elements of their story into their games. Using a book the class has read as an example, talk about ways to include information about the characters, setting, and story. Brainstorm possible names for a game based on the book. Explain that players should be able to play the game without having read the book. In other words, the game should not test the players' knowledge of the book.

Once students have finished their games, set aside blocks of time to play the games in small groups.

Name: _____ Date: _____

Design a Game

Imagine that you work for a toy company and you have been asked to design a board game. The game should be based on the book you just finished and should include information about the characters, setting, and story. When you have finished your game, your classmates will have a chance to play it.

DUE DATES
Book approved
_____
Book finished
_____
Project finished
_____

MATERIALS

cardboard or posterboard, markers, glue, construction paper, dice, index cards or paper, playing pieces, lined paper, small resealable plastic bags, brass fasteners or paper clips

DIRECTIONS

1 Find a science fiction or fantasy book that interests you and is at an appropriate reading level for you. Have your book approved by your teacher.

Book Title: _____

Author: _____

2 Write the characters' names, along with a sentence identifying each one.

_____

_____

_____

_____

_____

3 In a sentence or two, describe the setting of the story.

_____

_____

_____

_____

{4} Briefly describe the main conflict or problem. Explain how the conflict was resolved.

_____

_____

_____

_____

_____

{5} Think about how you can design a board game based on all or some of the information above (characters, setting, conflict, and resolution). Keep in mind that players should be able to play the game even if they have not read the book. Consider these questions:

☼ How is the game played? What are the rules?

_____

_____

☼ What will the game board and playing pieces look like?

_____

_____

☼ How does someone win? (Will they reach **FINISH** first? Will they collect the most points along the way?)

_____

_____

☼ Will you use a spinner, cards, or dice in your game?

_____

_____

{6} On a separate sheet of paper, sketch the game board. Test your game to make sure it works before you make a final copy of the game board.

{7} Write clear directions explaining how to play it. (You will find that the simpler the game is, the easier it will be to play.) Number each step in the directions.

{8} Make a final copy of your game board and any other parts (cards, spinner, playing pieces, and so on). Design the board so that it is colorful, neat, and attractive. Write the title and author of the book somewhere on the game board, along with your own name and a fun-sounding name for the game.

24 Ready-to-Go Genre Book Reports ✷ Scholastic Professional Books

Name: _____ Date: _____

Science Fiction/Fantasy

Design a Game

Book Title: _____

	POSSIBLE POINTS	POINTS EARNED
(1) Was your book approved by the due date?	5	
(2) Did you hand in your project on time?	10	
(3) Was your game neat, colorful, and attractive?	15	
(4) Was your game based on your book?	20	
(5) Did you write clear directions for your game?	20	
(6) Is your game playable? (Does it work?)	15	
(7) Did you give your game a fun name?	5	
(8) Are the spelling, punctuation, and grammar correct?	10	

Comments: _____

_____

_____

_____

_____

_____

Travel Brochure

GUIDELINES

Objective: Students choose an interesting setting from their book and create a travel brochure that advertises this place.

Show students several travel brochures and discuss the kinds of information presented in each. If possible, show brochures for large cities and small towns. Ask students to describe the writing style. How are the brochures designed to attract tourists? Challenge students to think of additional information that these brochures could have included to appeal to visitors.

Students first describe the setting of the book. If there is more than one setting, have them choose the most interesting one. Students brainstorm the attractions in this place, thinking about what the characters do there for fun.

If students are stuck, help them think of ways to creatively advertise a place that might not offer as much to do. Is it a place to relax and enjoy the peace and quiet? Explain that students can use events from the book in their brochures—for example, tourists could visit the famous white picket fence in *The Adventures of Tom Sawyer.*

Show students how to fold a sheet of paper into thirds to create their brochure. Before they begin their final draft, have them plan what they will write and draw. Encourage students to be creative as they think of ways to advertise this setting. The less tourist attractions a place offers, the more creative students can be in finding a way to advertise it.

Make a travel display with the brochures, and invite students to read their classmates' work. If you would like students to present their brochures, have them plan a short two-minute commercial for their setting.

Science Fiction/Fantasy

Travel Brochure

Do you think tourists would enjoy visiting the setting of the book you read? What attractions would they find in this place? What could they do for entertainment? What could they see and learn about? Imagine that you work for a travel agency and you have been asked to design a brochure to advertise this place. (If your book has more than one setting, choose the most unusual and interesting one.)

DUE DATES
Book approved
_____
Book finished
_____
Project finished
_____

MATERIALS

markers or colored pencils, 8 $\frac{1}{2}$- by 11-inch plain white paper (or larger)

DIRECTIONS

1. Find a science fiction or fantasy book that interests you and is at an appropriate reading level for you. Have your book approved by your teacher.

   Book Title: _____

   Author: _____

2. Describe the setting (time and place) of the book. If the book is set in more than one place, describe the most interesting or unusual one.

   _____

   _____

   _____

   _____

3. What activities do the characters do here for fun? What places are there to visit? What is there to learn about?

   _____

   _____

   _____

   _____

(4) Does this seem like an interesting place to visit? Why or why not?

_____

_____

_____

_____

(5) Hold a sheet of paper horizontally and fold the paper in thirds to form a brochure. First, fold the third on the right. Then fold the third on the left.

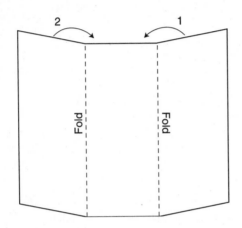

(6) On the front flap of the brochure, write the name of the place. If it does not have a specific name in the book, make up a name that sounds interesting. Illustrate the front flap with one or two of the main attractions of this place. You might add a sentence or two to entice travelers to read your brochure. Write the title and author somewhere on the front of the brochure.

(7) Plan the inside of the brochure before you begin writing or drawing. Include as many attractions as you can. Write reasons that travelers would want to visit each attraction. If there is not a lot to see or do in this setting, be creative and think about how you could make this place sound appealing to tourists.

(8) On the back panel, write a few paragraphs to provide any additional information that might persuade travelers to visit. Also explain interesting events from the book that took place in this setting. At the bottom, write "For additional information on (name of place), contact (your name)."

24 Ready-to-Go Genre Book Reports ✳ Scholastic Professional Books

Name: _____   Date: _____

Science Fiction/Fantasy

Travel Brochure

Book Title: _____

	POSSIBLE POINTS	POINTS EARNED
(1) Was your book approved on time?	5	
(2) Did you hand in your project on time?	10	
(3) Did you complete steps 2–4 on the directions sheet?	10	
(4) Did you complete each part of your brochure?	30	
(5) Is your brochure neat, colorful, and attractive?	10	
(6) Did you include thoughtful and convincing information?	25	
(7) Are the spelling, punctuation, and grammar correct?	10	

Comments: _____

_____

_____

_____

_____

_____

_____

_____

Write a Screenplay

| GUIDELINES |

Objective: *Students choose a scene from their science fiction or fantasy books and rewrite it as a scene for a movie screenplay.*

If possible, show students examples of movie screenplays or scripts for plays. Discuss the use of dialogue as well as other elements of a movie screenplay. Ask students to think about what directions the writer might include. How might they write directions for the actors? How do they describe what the camera will be filming?

Have students think about the elements of a good movie scene as they choose the part of the book they will rewrite. Write the following on the board:

- ✿ setting
- ✿ characters
- ✿ dialogue
- ✿ action
- ✿ special effects

Discuss how these elements contribute to a scene. Students might want to choose an action scene or one with interesting dialogue. Explain to students that if the scene in the book includes dialogue, they should adapt the dialogue so that they are not just copying it. They might make it shorter or they might add to it. They should write the dialogue so that it sounds like the characters are speaking. It will help to read their scripts aloud as they are writing.

When students have completed their final drafts, set aside time for them to work with small groups and act out their scenes. After they have practiced, have each group perform for the class.

24 Ready-to-Go Genre Book Reports ✽ Scholastic Professional Books

Science Fiction/Fantasy

Write a Screenplay

You have been asked to adapt a scene from your book into a scene for a movie. Choose a scene that you think would lend itself well to the format of a screenplay. You'll need to include dialogue and directions for the actors.

DUE DATES
Book approved
_____
Book finished
_____
Project finished
_____

MATERIALS

lined paper

DIRECTIONS

(1) Find a science fiction or fantasy book that interests you and is at an appropriate reading level for you. Have your book approved by your teacher.

Book Title: _____

Author: _____

(2) Choose a scene from the book to rewrite as a scene for a movie. Think about what makes a good movie scene, such as action, drama, dialogue, and special effects.

(3) Write a summary of what happens in this scene in the book. Then, think about how you will change it to make it a scene for a movie.

_____

_____

_____

_____

_____

_____

(4) Write a rough draft of the movie scene. Include dialogue, making sure that it sounds like the characters. Include directions for the actors about how they should look and act. You might also include some directions for the people working the camera—for example: "The camera spans the crowd and zooms in on a woman holding a sign. The woman looks frustrated as she tries to make her way through the crowd."

(5) Read your scene aloud and then revise it. Write a final draft of your scene. It should be at least two pages long and should cover the entire scene from the book.

Name: _____   Date: _____

Science Fiction/Fantasy

Write a Screenplay

Book Title: _____

	POSSIBLE POINTS	POINTS EARNED
(1) Was your book approved by the due date?	5	
(2) Did you hand in your project on time?	10	
(3) Did you write a rough draft?	10	
(4) Did you revise and write a final draft?	20	
(5) Is your scene complete and at least two pages long?	15	
(6) Did you include dialogue and directions for the actors?	15	
(7) Is your scene well written and interesting?	15	
(8) Are the spelling, punctuation, and grammar correct?	10	

Comments: _____

_____

_____

_____

_____

_____

Photo Album

GUIDELINES

Objective: *Students create a construction paper photo album of important people, places, events, or objects from a nonfiction book. Students write captions explaining the significance of the photos.*

Ask students to imagine that they have just taken a journey to the setting of their book (this may involve time travel). They visited the places in the book, witnessed the events, and met the characters. While they were there, they snapped pictures the entire time, like a photojournalist trying to capture every detail. Now they've returned home and they need to sort through all of their photos. They will choose the four most important photos.

The four photos should show what students believe are the most important aspects of their book. Students will then draw the four photos. They may need to do some research to find out what type of clothes were worn, what the landscape looked like, and so on. If their books include photographs or illustrations, students can use these as a reference.

Explain to students what a caption is. For each photo, students write a caption that is at least three sentences long. In the caption, students explain why the image in the photo is so important in the book. Finally, they mount the photos and captions in a construction paper album.

Make a classroom display of the albums. Have children each choose one or two photos to present to the class. Encourage classmates to ask the presenters questions about the books they've read.

Nonfiction

Photo Album

Imagine that you are a photojournalist who took
photographs of everything in your book. Choose four of
these photos to include in an album. The photos should
show the most important people, places, events, or objects
from the story. You will draw the photos and write a
caption for each.

DUE DATES

Book approved

_____

Book finished

_____

Project finished

_____

MATERIALS

four 3- by 5-inch index cards (or white paper cut to that size or
larger), large sheets of construction paper, markers or crayons,
glue or tape

DIRECTIONS

(1) Find a nonfiction book that interests you and is at an appropriate reading level for
you. Have your book approved by your teacher.

Book Title: _____

Author: _____

(2) Make a list of the most important people, places, events, and objects in the book.

_____

_____

_____

_____

(3) Choose the four most important or interesting items on your list. Draw and color an
illustration of each one to create a "photo."

(4) Write an interesting caption to describe each photo. Each caption should be at
least three sentences. In the caption, explain why the image shown is important in
the book.

(5) Fold a sheet of construction paper in half, like a book. On the front, write a title for
your album. Include the book title, author, and your name.

(6) Open the album and glue the photos inside. Glue a caption beneath each one.

24 Ready-to-Go Genre Book Reports ✫ Scholastic Professional Books

Name: _____   Date: _____

Nonfiction

Photo Album

Book Title: _____

	POSSIBLE POINTS	POINTS EARNED
(1) Did you have your book approved on time?	5	
(2) Did you hand in your project on time?	10	
(3) Did you draw four pictures of important people, places, events, or objects from your book?	20	
(4) Did you write captions that were at least three sentences?	15	
(5) Did your captions explain the importance of the photos?	15	
(6) Did you display the photos and captions in an album?	10	
(7) Is your project neat and colorful?	10	
(8) Did you write a title on the front and include the book title, author, and your name?	5	
(9) Are the spelling, punctuation, and grammar correct?	10	

Comments: _____
_____
_____

E-mail a Friend

GUIDELINES

Objective: *Students write two e-mail messages. First, they write a message from a friend or family member asking questions about the book. Then, they write a message answering the questions and persuading the friend or family member to read the book.*

Provide examples of persuasive writing. Read some of these together and discuss how the writers tried to persuade readers. Ask students to identify which parts were convincing and which parts were not. Look at the use of specific examples.

For this project, students write two e-mail messages. If e-mail is unavailable, they can simply write an e-mail heading at the top of a sheet of paper. First, students think of a friend or family member who might enjoy the book they read. Then, they imagine they are the friend or family member and write questions that he or she might have about the book.

Students write a rough draft of their answers, as well as any other reasons to convince their friend to read the book. As they write, have students recall the techniques the writers used in the examples you studied. Remind them to include specific examples. Also point out that they know the person they are writing to, and they should tailor their recommendation for that person. (For example, a student could write: "You always talk about how much you like camping, so I think you would really enjoy the scene in which…)

As an alternative, you could have students work with a partner and write to each other. Each student would write a letter of questions to the other; the recipient would then write a response.

Nonfiction

E-mail a Friend

In this project, you'll write an e-mail message to a friend who might enjoy the nonfiction book you just finished. First, put yourself in your friend's shoes and think of the questions he or she might ask you about the book. Then, you'll write an e-mail message answering those questions and persuading the friend to read the book. (If e-mail is unavailable, you can write your messages on paper.)

DUE DATES
Book approved
_____
Book finished
_____
Project finished
_____

| MATERIALS |

lined paper

| DIRECTIONS |

(1) Find a nonfiction book that interests you and is at an appropriate reading level for you. Have your book approved by your teacher.

Book Title: _____

Author: _____

(2) Think of a friend (or relative) who might enjoy this book. What might this friend want to know about the book before he or she reads it? What might your friend want to know about the writing style, plot, characters, story, and so on? Write an e-mail message to yourself from your friend, asking you about the book. Include at least four thoughtful questions. Print the message to hand in to the teacher. (You do not need to send an actual e-mail. You can simply write it on paper.) Write this information at the top of the page and fill it in:

To: _____

From: _____

Date sent: _____

Subject: _____

Message: _____

_____

_____

_____

_____

_____

_____

_____

_____

{3} Before you write back to your friend, organize your thoughts. Write a rough draft responding to your friend's questions and providing any other reasons that your friend would enjoy the book. Include specifics, but don't give away the ending.

{4} Revise your rough draft and then write a final draft. Either print the actual e-mail message or fill in this information at the top of a sheet of paper:

To: _____

From: _____

Date sent: _____

Subject: _____

Message: _____

_____

_____

_____

_____

_____

_____

Name: _____ Date: _____

Nonfiction

E-mail a Friend

Book Title: _____

	POSSIBLE POINTS	POINTS EARNED
(1) Was your book approved by the due date?	5	
(2) Did you hand in your project on time?	10	
(3) Did you write a message with at least four thoughtful questions about the book?	15	
(4) Did you write a rough draft of your response?	10	
(5) Did you revise your rough draft?	10	
(6) Did you write an effective persuasive letter that answered the questions?	30	
(7) Did you include specific examples from the book?	10	
(8) Are the spelling, punctuation, and grammar correct?	10	

Comments: _____

_____

_____

_____

_____

_____

Souvenirs

Objective: Students create or design four souvenirs that represent important aspects of a nonfiction book.

Ask students to explain what a souvenir is. Have they collected any souvenirs from places they've visited? What did the souvenirs look like, and how did they represent each place? If students were asked to create souvenirs for their hometown, what would they make? How would these objects represent the place? If possible, bring in souvenirs from various places or invite students to show some that they have collected. (Note: If students' nonfiction books deal with serious topics, such as slavery, have students complete a different project that would be more appropriate.)

Have students list the key places and events in their nonfiction book. After they list these, they choose the four that are most important in the book. Students write a paragraph on the importance of each and then design a souvenir of it. They do not have to create the souvenir (although they can if materials are available). They might design a T-shirt, key chain, paperweight, mug, magnet, statuette, postcard, and so on.

Once students have finished, create a class "gift shop" where students can display their projects. Place the written description beside each souvenir.

To create this project, a piece of paper was decorated and taped to a mug.

Nonfiction

Souvenirs

Have you ever bought a souvenir to remind you of a place you've visited? After you finish your nonfiction book, you'll choose four important places or events from it. For each place or event, you'll explain its importance and design a souvenir.

⎮ MATERIALS ⎰

> 3- by 5-inch index cards (or paper cut to that size), white paper, markers or colored pencils

⎮ DIRECTIONS ⎰

DUE DATES

Book approved

_____

Book finished

_____

Poster finished

_____

1) Find a nonfiction book that interests you and is at an appropriate reading level for you. Have your book approved by your teacher.

Book Title: _____

Author: _____

2) List the important places and events in the book. Write a sentence about each, explaining why it is important. Use the back of this sheet if you need more room.

_____

_____

_____

3) Circle the four items on the list that you feel are the most important in the book. Design a souvenir to represent each of the circled items. Think about the souvenirs you've seen in gift shops: T-shirts, key chains, paperweights, mugs, magnets, statuettes, postcards, bumper stickers, and so on. Sketch your design and then draw and color a final copy. Draw each one on a separate sheet of paper.

4) Next, consider the following questions: Why did you choose the four items that you circled? What did you learn about them in your book? Why are they important to remember? Why should others learn about them? How do your souvenirs represent the places or events that you chose? Write a paragraph that explains the significance of each.

5) Revise each paragraph and then copy a final version onto an index card (one index card per souvenir).

Name: _____ Date: _____

Nonfiction

Souvenirs

Book Title: _____

	POSSIBLE POINTS	POINTS EARNED
(1) Was your book approved by the due date?	5	
(2) Did you hand in your project on time?	10	
(3) Did you list important places and events and write a sentence about each?	10	
(4) Did you design four souvenirs?	20	
(5) Did you write a rough draft of your four paragraphs?	10	
(6) Did you revise and write a final copy?	15	
(7) Did your paragraphs explain the importance of each place or event?	10	
(8) Is your writing thoughtful and informative?	10	
(9) Are the spelling, punctuation, and grammar correct?	10	

Comments: _____

_____

_____

_____

Test Time

Objective: Students create a test and answer key based on their nonfiction book.

Ask students which they think is harder: writing a test or taking one. Explain that with this assignment, they'll have a chance to find out.

Review the different kinds of questions that appear on tests:

- essay
- multiple choice
- fill in the blank
- matching information
- true or false
- analogies

Ask students which questions they find the most and least difficult. Explain that they should include several types of questions in the test they will create and that they should also write an answer key for it. (You might offer extra credit for including and answering an essay question.)

After students have written information about their book, they decide which types of questions they wish to use. Point out that it's easiest to create the answer key as they write the test. Encourage them to refer to their books while they are making up questions and especially while they are writing the answers. Explain that they should ask questions about different aspects of the book.

If students have read the same book, you might have them take one another's tests. Have students grade their own papers, using the answer keys that their classmates created.

Name: _____   Date: _____

Test Time

It's your turn to be the teacher! After you finish your nonfiction book, you'll make up a test about it. Your test should include a few different sections, such as true/false, multiple choice, matching, and fill in the blank questions.

MATERIALS

lined paper

DIRECTIONS

DUE DATES
Book approved
_____
Book finished
_____
Project finished
_____

{1} Find a nonfiction book that interests you and is at an appropriate reading level for you. Have your book approved by your teacher.

Book Title: _____

Author: _____

{2} What is the setting (time and place) of your book? If there are several places in your book, list the most important ones.

_____

_____

_____

_____

_____

{3} List the most important people in your book and write a sentence or two about each one. (Use a separate sheet of paper if you need more space.)

_____

_____

_____

_____

_____

_____

24 Ready-to-Go Genre Book Reports ✳ Scholastic Professional Books

(4) Think about the important events that took place. List five of them and briefly explain why they were important.

_____

_____

_____

_____

_____

_____

_____

_____

(5) Now, use this and other information you recall from the book to make up a test. This test should not be extremely difficult. It should test whether someone has read the book and remembers the most important information. Include at least two different kinds of questions, such as true/false, fill in the blank, multiple choice, or matching. Write at least 15 questions. Make sure you ask questions about all aspects of the book: setting, characters, conflict, resolution, as well as the beginning, middle, and end of the story.

(6) Write a neat final copy of your test, numbering questions and labeling sections.

(7) On a separate sheet of paper, write an answer key. Make sure to check that your answers are correct.

Name: _____ Date: _____

Nonfiction

Test Time

Book Title: _____

	POSSIBLE POINTS	POINTS EARNED
1) Did you have your book approved on time?	5	
2) Did you hand in your project on time?	10	
3) Did you complete steps 2–4 on the directions sheet?	10	
4) Did you include at least 15 questions and two types of questions?	20	
5) Did you ask questions about several different aspects of the book?	20	
6) Did you create an accurate answer key?	15	
7) Is your project neat and organized (numbered and labeled)?	10	
8) Are the spelling, punctuation, and grammar correct?	10	

Comments: _____

_____

_____

_____

_____

Detective on the Case

Objective: Students act as detectives and file a case report based on their mystery. Their job is to report information such as setting, characters, clues, conflict, and resolution.

This activity will help students understand the characteristics of mysteries. They'll discover that quite a bit of the information is included to throw the reader off track as he or she is trying to figure out the mystery. Discuss the difference between real clues and false clues. A real clue helps the reader put the pieces together to reveal the solution to the mystery. A false clue makes the reader believe something other than the truth. At the end of the mystery, the reader discovers which clues were real and which were false. (Sometimes this information is revealed along the way.)

Students will notice a similar pattern with the characters as with the clues. Most likely, all of the characters acted suspicious at one time during the story. And perhaps the character that seemed the most innocent turned out to be the villain!

To show their understanding of the story, students write a description of how the case was solved. The most complicated part of a mystery is often the resolution, so this is an important part of the assignment.

Encourage students to make their projects look like official reports by designing their own case report forms and making up a name for their detective agency. They should include the name of the agency at the top of the form.

CLUES R US
Official Case Report

Case: Spider Kane and the Mystery Under the May-Apple by Mary Pope Osborne.

Location: The Cottage Garden and the Dark Swamp

Mystery: Mimi has been kidnapped and Leon tries to find her.

Characters:
La Mère Leafwing – Leon's mother. She dislikes Mimi from the start.
Leon Leafwing – A butterfly who tries to find Mimi.
Mimi – A new butterfly in the garden with a secret past.
Walter Dogtick – He used to be friends with La Mère. He was seen near Mimi's home carrying a large sack.
Spider Kane – A clever detective.
Emperor Moth – Ruler of the Dark Swamp, a criminal

Clues:
Stolen crown, book, and scarf – All were props used to trick Leon.
Message scratched in dirt – Also used to trick Leon and make him think Emperor Moth kidnapped Mimi.
Strange voice at campsite – This was the Hawk. They were discussing Leon.

Case Solved: Mimi was not really kidnapped. They made up the whole story to test Leon's courage and see if he could join the Order of MOTH. This is Spider Kane's group that helps other creatures in danger.

Detective Maria Berrios
Signature

December 12
Date

Detective on the Case

You've just landed a job as a detective! Now that the mystery in your book has been solved, your job is to file an official case report for your agency's records. You'll need to review the case and accurately fill in the information. Make the report look as official as you can by designing your own case report form. Be sure it includes the information listed below.

DUE DATES
Book approved
_____
Book finished
_____
Project finished
_____

MATERIALS

lined paper

DIRECTIONS

(1) Find a mystery that interests you and is at an appropriate reading level for you. Have your book approved by your teacher.

    Book Title: _____

    Author: _____

(2) At the top of your case report, write the name of your detective agency, the book title, and author. Then, write the location and the approximate time of the mystery (in other words, the setting).

(3) Next, write a brief description of the mystery. What was the problem? What needed to be solved?

(4) Look through the book to find clues that helped solve the mystery. Make a list of at least three of them. Beside each, write the information the clue revealed in the end.

(5) Who was involved? Make a list of the main characters. Beside each character, note any suspicious behavior that occurred at any point in the story. Write whether any additional information was revealed about each character at the end of the story.

(6) Finally, describe how the mystery was solved. If any detectives deserve special mention, explain why here.

(7) Sign and date your report, and pass it in to the chief detective (your teacher).

Name: _____   Date: _____

Mystery

Detective on the Case

Book Title: _____

	POSSIBLE POINTS	POINTS EARNED
{1} Was your book approved on time?	5	
{2} Did you hand in your project on time?	10	
{3} Did you describe the setting?	10	
{4} Did you describe the mystery?	15	
{5} Did you list and write about at least three clues?	15	
{6} Did you list the characters and any suspicious behavior?	15	
{7} Did you explain how the mystery was solved?	20	
{8} Are the spelling, punctuation, and grammar correct?	10	

Comments: _____

_____

_____

_____

_____

_____

Setting Map

Objective: Students choose a setting from the story and draw a map of it, labeling important places.

Ask students to define the term *setting.* Lead them to the understanding that setting includes both time and place. Ask them if their books have one setting or more than one. Did the book take place in several locations and over an extended period of time?

Discuss the importance of setting in a mystery. Explain that settings provide important information. Information about where events occur helps the characters and the reader try to solve the mystery. The setting also creates an atmosphere that sets the mood for the story.

Ask students the following questions:

✿ Why might atmosphere be especially important in a mystery.?

✿ What is a typical atmosphere for this genre?

✿ Does your book have this type of atmosphere?

✿ How does an author create a particular atmosphere?

Have students look through their books to find descriptions of setting that create a mood. You might have students work in small groups to share descriptions from their books.

For this project, students first list the important places in their book. They then choose one place to represent on a map. They should choose an important place that is described in detail in the book. Encourage students to look in their books for specific descriptions so that they can include as much detail on their map as possible. They can be creative in how they indicate important places—for example, they might put a thumbprint in each place on the map to indicate a place where a clue was discovered.

Challenge students to make their maps reflect the mood of the story. They might do this through their drawings, colors, writing style, and title. Display the maps in your classroom, and have each student describe what the map shows (without giving away the ending of the book).

Mystery

Setting Map

For this project, you'll choose an important setting and make a map of it. On your map, you'll indicate where events took place and include other noteworthy information. Include illustrations and labels.

DUE DATES

Book approved

_____

Book finished

_____

Project finished

_____

MATERIALS

large sheet of white or light-colored paper, markers or colored pencils

DIRECTIONS

(1) Find a mystery that interests you and is at an appropriate reading level for you. Have your book approved by your teacher.

Book Title: _____

Author: _____

(2) Make a list of the important places in your book. Write a sentence or two explaining the significance of each.

_____

_____

_____

_____

_____

(3) You will make a map of one place on your list. Choose a place that is important to the story—perhaps where the most exciting event occurred. If a place is important, the author probably provided information about what it looked like.

(4) Look in your book for descriptions of this place. Take notes on the details.

_____

_____

_____

_____

_____

{5} In the box below, sketch what you will include on your map. Draw pictures to show important places and note events that took place there.

(blank box)

{6} Draw your final copy on a large sheet of white or light-colored paper. Color your illustrations and label each place on the map. Write the name of the place and the important events that occurred there.

{7} Give your map a title and write it at the top. Write the book title, author, and your name on the map.

24 Ready-to-Go Genre Book Reports ✳ Scholastic Professional Books

Name: _____ Date: _____

Mystery

Setting Map

Book Title: _____

	POSSIBLE POINTS	POINTS EARNED
1 Was your book approved by the due date?	5	
2 Did you hand in your project on time?	10	
3 Did you list the important places and write about each?	5	
4 Did you take notes on the place you chose for your map?	5	
5 Did you sketch your map?	5	
6 Was your map complete and detailed?	20	
7 Did your map include illustrations?	20	
8 Did your map include labels of places and the events that occurred there?	15	
9 Did you give your map a title?	5	
10 Are the spelling, punctuation, and grammar correct?	10	

Comments: _____

_____

_____

New Ending

GUIDELINES

Objective: Students write a different ending for a mystery.

This creative writing assignment allows students to analyze the resolution of a mystery and write their own ending. As they read their mysteries, students will most likely believe that there will be a different outcome. This is their chance to write the ending that they anticipated.

To get students started on this project, ask questions such as:

✷ Did you think the mystery would end differently and why?

✷ Could the clues have pointed to a different conclusion?

✷ Did characters who acted suspicious turn out to be innocent?

✷ Did characters who seemed innocent turn out to be suspicious?

Have students find the part in the book that they will use as their starting point. Explain that the transition should be smooth from the author's writing to their own. You might have students copy a paragraph from the book at the beginning of their writing assignment. Then, encourage them to write in a style similar to the author's.

After students have written a rough draft, you may want to have them revise their writing in class. Ask students to read their drafts and make sure that they have thoroughly explained their new ending. Are there any unanswered questions? If so, students should explain anything that is still unclear.

Set aside a time for students to read aloud their final drafts to the class and answer any questions their classmates might have. Remind them not to give away the real ending.

24 Ready-to-Go Genre Book Reports ✷ Scholastic Professional Books

Mystery

New Ending

Did the ending of your mystery surprise you? How did you think it would end? Imagine that you are the author of the mystery and your editor has asked you to rewrite the ending. How would you change it?

DUE DATES
Book approved
_____
Book finished
_____
Project finished
_____

MATERIALS

lined paper

DIRECTIONS

(1) Find a mystery that interests you and is at an appropriate reading level for you. Have your book approved by your teacher.

Book Title: _____

Author: _____

(2) Think about how the book ended. If you could go back to the point in the book before the mystery was solved and rewrite the ending, what would happen? How would things have turned out differently? Find the part of the book that you will use as a starting point. Write the page number of your starting point. Briefly describe what has just occured in the book.

_____

_____

_____

_____

(3) Write a rough draft of your new ending. It should be at least one page.

(4) Read your rough draft and make sure it solves the mystery in a way that makes sense. Did you tie up all the loose ends? Revise your rough draft to make your writing stronger. (Add dialogue and description. Change passive verbs to active verbs. Check your spelling, punctuation, and grammar.)

(5) Write a neat copy of your final draft, and add a title.

Name: _____   Date: _____

Mystery

New Ending

Book Title: _____

	POSSIBLE POINTS	POINTS EARNED
(1) Did you have your book approved by the due date?	5	
(2) Did you hand in your project on time?	10	
(3) Did you write a rough draft that was at least one page?	15	
(4) Did you revise your rough draft?	15	
(5) Did you write a neat final draft?	15	
(6) Does your new ending make sense?	15	
(7) Is your writing thoughtful and interesting?	15	
(8) Are the spelling, punctuation, and grammar correct?	10	

Comments: _____

_____

_____

_____

_____

_____

24 Ready-to-Go Genre Book Reports ☆ Scholastic Professional Books

Character Cards

Objective: Students create at least five character cards. Each card includes an illustration and important information about a character.

To get students started on this project, display baseball cards and explain that students will make similar cards for the characters in their book. Ask students what information they would include on these cards, and list their suggestions on the board.

Discuss the role that characters play in a mystery and the idea that in this genre characters often aren't who they seem to be. Ask students to think about the characters in the mystery they have read. Pose the following questions:

☼ How does the author portray the characters?

☼ What does the author want the reader to believe about each one?

☼ Did students find any hints about the characters along the way that helped reveal their true role in the mystery?

Encourage students to think about these questions and answer them in a general way so that they do not give away the endings of their mysteries. If several students have read the same book, they might discuss these questions in a small group.

Encourage students to look up information in their book as they fill in their cards. As an alternative to drawing a picture, have students look through old magazines and catalogs and cut out pictures that fit the characters' descriptions.

Tabitha-Ruth "Turtle" Wexler

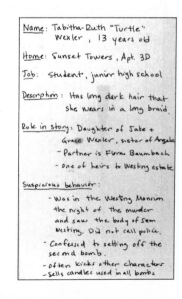

Name: Tabitha-Ruth "Turtle" Wexler, 13 years old

Home: Sunset Towers, Apt. 3D

Job: Student, junior high school

Description: Has long dark hair that she wears in a long braid.

Role in story: Daughter of Jake + Grace Wexler, sister of Angela
- Partner is Flora Baumbach
- One of heirs to Westing estate

Suspicious behavior:
- Was in the Westing Mansion the night of the murder and saw the body of Sam Westing. Did not call police.
- Confessed to setting off the second bomb.
- Often kicks other characters
- Sells candles used in all bombs

Mystery

Character Cards

Here's a way to keep track of all the characters—make trading cards for them. These cards will look like baseball cards but will show different kinds of information.

MATERIALS

5- by 8-inch index cards (or paper cut to this size)

DIRECTIONS

(1) Find a mystery that interests you and is at an appropriate reading level for you. Have your book approved by your teacher.

Book Title: _____

Author: _____

(2) List the characters here.

_____

_____

_____

(3) Circle the characters that are most important to the story. (Even a character that seems to have a small part might be very important in the end.)

(4) Make a character card for each of the characters you circled. (You should make at least five cards.) On one side of the index card, draw and color a picture of the character. Write the character's name below or above your picture.

(5) On the back of each card, include the following information. You may need to look up some of this information in your book. If you can't find the exact information, write "Information not available."

    ✿ Name and approximate age

    ✿ Home

    ✿ Occupation (job)

    ✿ Physical description (what the character looks like)

    ✿ Role in story (how the character is involved in the mystery)

    ✿ Suspicious or unusual behavior

Name: _____   Date: _____

Mystery

Character Cards

Book Title: _____

	POSSIBLE POINTS	POINTS EARNED
(1) Did you have your book approved by the due date?	5	
(2) Did you hand in your project on time?	10	
(3) Did you make a list of the characters?	10	
(4) Did you make at least five character cards?	25	
(5) Did you draw a picture on one side of each?	20	
(6) Did you complete the information on the other side?	20	
(7) Are the spelling, punctuation, and grammar correct?	10	

Comments: _____

_____

_____

_____

_____

_____

_____

Story Quilt

| GUIDELINES |

Objective: Students create a quilt depicting symbols from the story. Students explain the significance of each.

This project helps students identify and understand symbolism in literature. Start by discussing objects that are important to students. Help students understand the difference between objects they like (video games, shoes, and so on) and those that might hold a deeper significance. Explain that a symbol is an object that represents something important. It symbolizes something else that is more meaningful than the object itself. Discuss examples that students provide to discover what the objects symbolize. You might also use examples from books that you have read as a class.

Students will choose four important symbols from their book. They will create a simple paper quilt on which to draw the symbols. Explain that they are creating a story quilt because each symbol helps tell part of the story. If possible, provide wrapping paper for students to create patterned squares to add to their quilt. In the center they will write the title and author of their book, as well as their name.

To extend this activity, have students choose an additional symbol from their book and make a separate square for it with a picture and a brief explanation. Tape these together to form a class quilt. If desired, make a checkerboard pattern by attaching solid or patterned paper squares in between each student square.

Historical Fiction

Story Quilt

Can you think of any objects that have special meaning to you? Do they remind you of a person or an important event? Now, think about the historical fiction book that you read. Were there any significant objects in the story? In literature, these objects are called symbols. They are symbolic of something important. For this project, you'll make a quilt that shows four symbols from the book.

DUE DATES

Book approved

_____

Book finished

_____

Project finished

_____

MATERIALS

large square sheet of white construction paper, ruler, markers or colored pencils, scissors, wrapping paper (optional)

DIRECTIONS

1 Find a book of historical fiction that interests you and is at an appropriate reading level for you. Have your book approved by your teacher.

Book Title: _____

Author: _____

2 Measure and draw light pencil lines to divide the white paper square into thirds across and lengthwise. This will create nine equal squares for your paper quilt.

3 Look through your book to help you remember objects that were important to the story. These objects should represent something significant, like a person or an event. List at least six of them below.

_____

_____

_____

_____

(4) Circle four objects from the list that you would like to include on your quilt. Sketch each object in a box below.

(5) Write a few sentences explaining why each object is important. What does it symbolize or represent? Revise your sentences on a separate sheet of paper.

_____

_____

_____

_____

_____

_____

_____

(6) Locate the four squares in the corners of the quilt. Draw one object in each square. Leave room in the same square to copy your sentences about the object. It is a good idea to draw and write in pencil first and then trace over it with pen or thin marker.

(7) Write the title and author of the book in the center square.

(8) Cut the wrapping paper into squares that are the same size as those on the quilt. Glue a wrapping paper square in each of the blank squares. (If wrapping paper is not available, cut squares of colored paper and draw simple patterns or designs on them. Glue these in the blank squares.)

Name: _____   Date: _____

Historical Fiction

Story Quilt

Book Title: _____

	POSSIBLE POINTS	POINTS EARNED
(1) Was the book approved by the due date?	5	
(2) Did you hand in your project on time?	10	
(3) Did you list six important objects?	5	
(4) Did you draw four objects on your quilt?	20	
(5) Did you write a few sentences explaining the importance of each?	20	
(6) Did you write the title and author in the center?	10	
(7) Did you cover the remaining squares with paper?	10	
(8) Is your project neat and colorful?	10	
(9) Are the spelling, punctuation, and grammar correct?	10	

Comments: _____

_____

_____

_____

_____

Postcards

24 Ready-to-Go Genre Book Reports ✷ Scholastic Professional Books

| GUIDELINES |

Objective: *Students write and illustrate three postcards about an important character, place, and event in their book.*

Ask students to explain the difference between facts and opinions. Choose topics of interest, such as sports or television shows, and have students think of facts and opinions about each. Write these on the board and ask students to explain what makes each a fact or opinion.

Have students choose the most interesting person, place, and event as the three topics for their postcards. They should come up with at least one fact and opinion about each topic. You may want them to come up with several to reiterate the difference between facts and opinions. You might extend this assignment and have children choose one of their opinions and then support it with three facts in a paragraph or short essay.

Students should choose whom they will write to and then write a message on each postcard that incorporates their facts and opinions. They will draw a picture on the back of each postcard to illustrate their topic.

Invite students to choose one of their postcards to read aloud to the class. Challenge classmates to identify the facts and opinions that they hear. Add the projects to a Postcard Museum (you could display the postcards on a tabletop or bulletin board). If you hang them on a bulletin board, use a piece of tape at the top of each postcard so that viewers can flip up the cards to see the other side. Have students brainstorm ideas to make the Postcard Museum a unique showcase.

Historical Fiction

Postcards

Have you ever received or sent a postcard? For this project, you'll write three postcards about your book to a friend or relative. You will choose an important person, character, and event to write about. In each postcard, you'll write both facts and opinions about your topic. Then you'll draw an illustration on the back of the postcard.

DUE DATES
Book approved
_____
Book finished
_____
Project finished
_____

MATERIALS

three 5- by 8-inch unlined index cards (or heavy white paper cut to that size), markers or colored pencils

DIRECTIONS

(1) Find a book of historical fiction that interests you and is at an appropriate reading level for you. Have your book approved by your teacher.

Book Title: _____

Author: _____

(2) Choose a topic for each of the three postcards. Your three topics should be an important person, place, and event from the story. List them below and briefly explain the significance of each. Then write the topics in the chart on the next page.

_____

_____

_____

_____

_____

_____

_____

_____

_____

_____

_____

_____

❋3❋ Think of at least one fact and one opinion about each topic. List these in the chart below. If you need more room, create a similar chart on a separate sheet of paper.

TOPIC	FACT	OPINION

❋4❋ Decide whom you will write to on each postcard. You could write to the same friend or relative for all of them, or you could choose a different person for each one. Write a rough draft of your message for each postcard, incorporating the facts and opinions from the chart. Include any other information about the book that would interest your friend or relative.

❋5❋ Revise your rough draft and then write your final draft on the cards. Don't forget to sign and address the postcards.

❋6❋ On the back of each postcard, draw the person, place, or event that you wrote about. (First, sketch them in the boxes below.) Write the book title and author as well as your name.

24 Ready-to-Go Genre Book Reports ❋ Scholastic Professional Books

Name: _____   Date: _____

Historical Fiction

Postcards

Book Title: _____

	POSSIBLE POINTS	POINTS EARNED
(1) Was your book approved on time?	5	
(2) Did you hand in your project on time?	10	
(3) Did you complete the chart?	10	
(4) Did you write a rough draft?	10	
(5) Did you revise your rough draft?	10	
(6) Did you include a fact and an opinion in each postcard?	15	
(7) Are your postcards well written and interesting?	15	
(8) Did you draw a picture on each postcard?	15	
(9) Are the spelling, punctuation, and grammar correct?	10	

Comments: _____

_____

_____

_____

_____

Comic Strip

⟩ GUIDELINES ⟩

Objective: Students create a comic strip to retell an important part of their historical fiction books.

Bring in the funny pages from a newspaper and any additional comic strips you think will provide a good example for students. Ask students to name the components and characteristics of a comic strip. Discuss the use of illustrations, characters, and speech balloons. Explain that the comic strips that students create do not need to be humorous. (If students' historical fiction books deal with serious subjects, such as slavery, have students complete a different project that would be more appropriate.)

Note in the examples that comic strips often use dialogue and action to tell a short story. Have students consider this as they choose the part of the story they will retell. After they have decided on a part of the book that would lend itself well to the comic strip format, students write a summary of that part of the book. Students then sketch their comic strip to make sure they can fit all of the information in about eight panels. If students find it too difficult to draw the characters, they can draw stick figures instead.

Make a class funny pages section with all of the completed projects. Fold large sheets of newsprint in half, like a newspaper. Add a heading at the top of each page that includes the name of the newspaper and the date. Attach the comic strips to the pages and display on a tabletop. Or you might display the comic strips on a bulletin board.

24 Ready-to-Go Genre Book Reports ✳ Scholastic Professional Books

Historical Fiction

Comic Strip

For this project, you'll create a comic strip based on a part of the historical fiction book you read. Your comic strip should include illustrations as well as text. Look at real comic strips for ideas.

DUE DATES

Book approved

_____

Book finished

_____

Project finished

_____

MATERIALS

large sheets of white construction paper, thin markers or colored pencils, ruler

DIRECTIONS

(1) Find a book of historical fiction that interests you and is at an appropriate reading level for you. Have your book approved by your teacher.

Book Title: _____

Author: _____

(2) Choose an important or exciting part of the book that you would like to retell in your comic strip. Find a part that will allow you to include action and dialogue. Write a one-paragraph summary of this part of the book.

(3) Refer to your summary as you sketch your comic strip. Decide what you will include in each panel. Your comic strip should include about eight panels in all. If you have difficulty drawing the characters, you may draw stick figures. Make sure to give them some identifiable characteristics so that the reader can tell them apart. Also make sure that the sequence of events is clear and easy to follow.

(4) Position a sheet of white construction paper horizontally and draw eight boxes of equal size. (You might need to make some larger and some smaller, depending on what you will include in each.) Draw and write in pencil first, then copy over with pen or thin marker. Keep the illustrations and text as neat as possible. Then, color your comic strip.

(5) Give your comic strip a title. Write your name, the book title, and the author's name on your project.

Name: _____ Date: _____

Historical Fiction

Comic Strip

Book Title: _____

	POSSIBLE POINTS	POINTS EARNED
(1) Was your book approved on time?	5	
(2) Did you hand in your project on time?	10	
(3) Did you choose an interesting or exciting part of the book?	10	
(4) Did you write a one-paragraph summary?	10	
(5) Did you complete your comic strip?	25	
(6) Does your comic strip effectively retell the selected part of the book?	10	
(7) Does your comic strip include illustrations and text?	10	
(8) Is your comic strip neat and easy to follow?	10	
(9) Are the spelling, punctuation, and grammar correct?	10	

Comments: _____

_____

_____

Time Line

GUIDELINES

Objective: *Students research the time period their book was set in and create a time line showing historical events that occurred during that era.*

Historical fiction lends itself well to research projects such as this. Reading a book of this genre helps students become more interested in the historical events of the time period in which the story was set. In addition, as students research the time period, they will gain a better understanding of the story.

It is important that students correctly identify the time period in which their book was set before they begin this project. Check students' work on step 2 to make sure they have written the correct time period. Students then begin research to determine which important events they would like to include.

After they have taken some preliminary notes, they should again meet with you to narrow or expand their time frames. If a student's book is set during one year, the student might show five to ten years on their time line. If a student's book spans 50 years, the student might show 15 to 25 years. The amount of time shown also depends on how much happened during that time period. If many important events occurred within a short period of time, students should make their time frames shorter (and vice versa).

Discuss the types of events students might include on their time lines. As a group, brainstorm a list of categories and write them on the board. The list might include the following:

- politics
- economics
- exploration
- inventions and technology
- famous people (accomplishments, dates of birth and death)

- sports and entertainment
- civil rights
- women's rights
- space travel

Encourage students to include some fun facts as well, such as the invention of the Hula-Hoop. These should be in addition to the ten important events.

Show students how to position large sheets of white paper horizontally and then cut across them. This will create long strips of paper that can be attached end to end. To make their time lines visually appealing, students should include illustrations and other decorations. The time lines should be colorful, informative, and easy to read.

Historical Fiction

Time Line

After you finish your book of historical fiction, you will research the time period in which your book is set. Based on your research, you'll then make a time line to show at least ten important events that occurred during that time period.

DUE DATES

Book approved

_____

Book finished

_____

Project finished

_____

MATERIALS

large sheets of white construction paper (cut in half to create long, horizontal strips), markers or colored pencils

DIRECTIONS

1 Find a book of historical fiction that interests you and is at an appropriate reading level for you. Have your book approved by your teacher.

Book Title: _____

Author: _____

2 Look through the book and determine when it was set. If it does not tell you the exact years, look up the dates of historical events that occurred in the book. Write the time period here, and briefly describe how you found out. Have your teacher check this step before you continue.

_____

_____

_____

_____

_____

_____

_____

3 You will create a time line about the period of time in which your book was set. Your time line should include at least ten important events, including any historical events that were mentioned in the book. Research this time period using the Internet, reference books, and other resources. Take notes on important events and the dates they happened.

24 Ready-to-Go Genre Book Reports ✹ Scholastic Professional Books

(4) Now that you are more knowledgeable about the time period, choose an exact time frame for your project. Discuss the time frame with your teacher before you continue. If many important events occurred during a short period of time, your time frame should be shorter. If not as many events occurred, your time frame should be longer.

(5) Sketch a rough draft of your time line. You should write one or two complete sentences for each event on the time line. Write your rough draft on the lines below. Add illustrations and other decorations to make your time line eye-catching and colorful.

1. _____

_____

2. _____

_____

3. _____

_____

4. _____

_____

5. _____

_____

6. _____

_____

7. _____

_____

8. _____

_____

9. _____

_____

10. _____

_____

Name: _____   Date: _____

Historical Fiction

Time Line

Book Title: _____

	POSSIBLE POINTS	POINTS EARNED
(1) Was your book approved on time?	5	
(2) Did you hand in your project on time?	10	
(3) Did you have a teacher check the dates in step 2?	5	
(4) Did you have a teacher approve the span of time you covered?	5	
(5) Did you include at least ten important events on your time line?	25	
(6) Did you write one or two complete sentences about each event?	15	
(7) Is your time line neat, colorful, and easy to read?	15	
(8) Did you include illustrations?	10	
(9) Are the spelling, punctuation, and grammar correct?	10	

Comments: _____

_____

_____

_____

Name: _____ Date: _____

Genre: _____

Project: _____

Book Title: _____

	POSSIBLE POINTS	POINTS EARNED
(1)		
(2)		
(3)		
(4)		
(5)		
(6)		
(7)		
(8)		
(9)		
(10)		

Comments: _____

_____

_____

_____

_____

Name: _____   Date: _____

Reading Log

DATE FINISHED	BOOK TITLE	AUTHOR	GENRE
1.			
2.			
3.			
4.			
5.			
6.			
7.			
8.			
9.			
10.			
11.			
12.			